Windows 10 2021 User Guide

I0003895

Get Started With

The All-Inclusive User Guide for

Beginners ✚ Tips for Experts to Help You

Steer Through

Ella Brown

Copyright © 2021 Ella Brown

Contents

Introduction

The best operating system produced by Microsoft is Windows 10. Despite being the best, it is also the most sophisticated. Although it comes with a simplistic interface, you need to have a better understanding to get maximum performance and get the utmost out of features like Edge browser, Cortana voice assistant, and other software. If you still make use of Windows 7 which is becoming obsolete, this guide will aid you to have a smooth transition to Windows 10.

Free way to upgrade to Windows 10 in 2020

1. Search for a Windows 7, 8, or 8.1 software copy together with it's key. If one is already installed on your computer, but you can't find it's key, you can make use of a free tool such as NirSoft's Product Key. This tool can extract the product key from the running PC software.

2.   You can make use of this moment to back up any of your important files before you continue.

3.   The next thing to do is to create a Windows 10 installer. To do this, go here to create the installer for Windows 10 then configure it. (Make use of your hardware of choice to create the installation media for a different computer). Make use of a USB flash drive if you want to install it from a USB flash drive or use an ISO file if you want to burn it to a DVD. Also, select the bit version, either 32 bit or 64 bit.

4.   Put in the media for installation, reboot the computer and press F2. This allows you to choose a different boot sequence so as to allow the DVD or USB flash drive to run

first. While on this, choose DVD or USB drive in the boot sequence to allow it boot before the hard disk.

5.   Restart your computer again.

6.   When the installation commences, you will be required to input your key. Input it here and click on Next.

How to Update Windows 10

An easy and efficient method of making your computer work better is by updating the software. Updating Windows 10 will give your computer the latest security patches, bug fixes, and other latest features.

Thankfully, Windows normally carries out system update automatically. What is needed of you to do is to reboot your system to ensure that the update is complete (check this guide for tips on how to paid update for up to 35 days). Even though automatic updates are convenient, there are times where you want to search for updates manually especially when you may have noticed a big.

Read our guide on what to do as a Windows 7 user as it nears its last days. Set up your system properly once the update is complete.

Below are some procedures to manually search for updates of Windows 10.

Method of updating Windows 10 manually

1. Click the Start or Windows button located at the bottom left corner of the screen.

2. Navigate to settings (symbolized with the gear icon).

3. Click the Update and Security icon

4. Click the Windows Update tab located in the sidebar (Circular arrows)

5. Click Check for updates. Any available updates will automatically download.

There is no need to worry if there are no updates available. This is because the page will also tell you if your system is not compatible. Also, you may see the message: "The Windows 10 May 2019 Update is on its way. We're offering this update to compatible devices, but your device isn't ready for it. Once your device is ready, you'll see the updates available on this page. There's nothing you need to do at this time."

Windows 10 will inform you with clear instructions if you are to restart your system (Note, your system will not have the latest updates till it has been rebooted). Learn install Windows 10 installation, how to tweak settings, add perform key and users, and other activities.

Some Windows 10 Settings to Modify

There are many exciting features such as a new Start menu and Cortana in the Windows 10 Operating system. However, you cant achieve the best performance with some of its default settings. Ranging from activating system protections to displaying file extensions, below are seven items worthy of modification for your newly acquired and newly setup system

Create a point of restoration / Activate System Protection

What will you do if your computer malfunctions as a result of bad software installation or a bad device driver? Ideally, you would want to revert the system to its previous restore point to take back the drivers, settings, and programs to the point where they worked well. By default, Windows 10 comes with disabled system protection. You have to set it up and set up the restore points using the instructions below.

1. Look in the Windows search box for "restore point".

2. From the results, launch "Create a restore point". There should be a list of available drives displayed.

3. Choose the system drive and click Configure. Usually, C: drive is the system drive. It also has the word "(System)" written after the name of the volume.

4. Turn on system protection by toggling Restore Settings. Then assign the maximum disk space for use by moving the slider. Finally, click Ok. We recommend that you leave 2 or 3 percent for the restore pint, although you can make use of 1 percent which is the lowest.

5. Click Create to immediately create an initial restore point.

6. When you are required to, give the initial restore point a name.

7. Finally, click Close.

Display Hidden Files and File Extensions

Windows 10 hides some file extensions. This makes them invisible as you are perusing through your files. For example, a web page you saved will be displayed as "homepage" instead of "homepage.htm" or "homepage.html" while your quarterly report will be displayed as "3dqreport" rather than "3dqreport.pptx"

In a move seen as simplifying the system for users, Microsoft has in the past been churning out systems with disabled extensions disabling extensions. This created more problems than solutions. As an instance, I had a problem when linking to a font file because I regarded it as "myfont.ttf" instead of "myfont.TTF."

While it means good, Microsoft has also hidden some files belonging to the operating system. What if you need these files for troubleshooting or edit and do not want to run into an error? Below is the way with which you can show hidden files and extensions in Windows 10.

1. Go to the control panel. You can reach there by pressing Windows + X and choosing Control Panel

2. Launch File Explorer Options. If the icon is not visible to you, change the view of the control panel to either small icons or large ones.

3. Go to the view tab

4. Toggle "Hidden files and folders" to "Show hidden files, folders, and drives."

5. Uncheck "Hide protected operating system files", "Hide empty drives, " and "Hide extensions for known file types"

6. Click Yes when you are prompted with a warning about unhiding protected files.

7. Click Ok.

Disable your User Account Control

Anytime you try installing software or change an important setting, Windows will display a dialog box, forcing you to click OK before you can continue. But is there any need for that? You can disable this feature to stop these dialog boxes.

1. Look in the search box for "user account control".

2. Enter "Change User Account Control settings."

3. Slide down the slider to "Never notify" then click Ok.

4. When prompted, click Yes.

Disable the Lock Screen

The lock screen may be an unnecessary decoration that makes you always swipe or click your screen before you can use it. Instead of making use of the lock screen on your computer, after which you will still be directed to the login page, while not just go straight to the login screen? To do this:

1. Enter the registry editor. Type Regedit in the Run box.

2. Go to HKEY_LOCAL_MACHINE\SOFTWARE\Policies\Microsoft\Windows.

3. Make a new registry key called Personalization if there is none already. Do this by right-clicking on the pane located at the right, then select Key.

5. Within the Personalization key, create a new DWORD value and name it NoLockScreen.

6.   Set the value data of NoLockScreen to 1. Double click on NoLockScreen, enter the value, and click Ok.

Change Your Default Browser

If you upgraded from Windows 7 or 8 to Windows 19, you will notice that the default browser is now Microsoft Edge, unlike before which was Firefox or Chrome. Though a bit faster than its rivals, Edge does not provide a better level of extensibility. You would want to change your browser if you are a Firefox or Chrome user.

1. Navigate to settings

2. Click System.

3. Select Default apps located at the left pane.

Delete the Windows. old Folder

After an upgrade from a Windows 7 or 8 to a Windows 10, there will still be a copy of the previous Windows version, in case you will still need to revert. However, those files, located in a folder called Windows.old, can take up to 15 to 16GB of disk space. If you have decided on staying with Windows 10, there is still no reason to keep that folder. Unfortunately, deleting this folder is not an easy task.

1. Go to the control panel. Press Windows + X to get there, then select the control panel.

2. Open Administrative Tools.

3. Launch Disk Cleanup

4. Click Ok. Ensure that you selected the C drive.

5. Click Clean up System Files.

6. Click Ok again

7 Check all the boxes on the "Files to delete" menu, especially "Temporary Windows Installation Files" and "Previous Windows Installations" then Click Ok.

7. Click Delete Files. This takes some minutes to complete

9. Click Yes to confirm.

This deletion process will take some minutes to be completed.

Use the following keyboard shortcuts to save you some clicks

11

Key combinations instead of making use of your mouse save you time. In Windows 10, these key combinations are numerous. They can be used to navigate around the operating system, launch new features like Cortana and also organize your desktop layout easily. Though you may already know some basic key combinations, the following are still important.

Cortana Shortcuts

Windows + C: Opens the speech prompt of Cortana

Windows + Q: Opens the Home View of Cortana and activates search by keyboard input or speech.

New Windows 10 Combinations

Windows Key + I: Opens Windows 10 settings

Windows Key + A: Opens Windows 10 notifications

Windows Key + Ctrl + F4: Closes current virtual desktop

Windows Key + Ctrl + D: Creates new virtual desktop

Windows Key + F1: Opens Edge and Searches "How do I get help in Windows 10" with Bing (formerly opens Help)

Windows Key + Ctrl + Left or Right: Switches between the virtual desktops

Windows Key + Print Screen Key: Creates a screenshot of the entire screen in the Photos app. You can find other screenshot key commands here.

Windows Standards

Windows Key + L: Locks your Windows 10 device

Windows Key: Shows the Windows 10 Start Menu

Windows Key + Tab: Launches Windows 10 Task View

Windows Key + Enter: Opens Narrator, a program that shows you tips and reads text for you.

Desktop Commands

Windows Key + X: Opens Start button context menu

Windows Key + Left, Right, Up or Down: Moves the active window around on your screen.

Left and Right moves the window to either side, taking up half of the screen.

Up and Down shrink the width to a quarter-size and move it to the corner.

Once you have placed it in the top corner by pressing Windows Key + Up, pressing it for the second time will make the window take up the entire screen.

If you pressed Windows Key + Down to place a window in the bottom corner, pressing it again will minimize the window.

Windows Key + D: Show Windows desktop (also possible with Windows Key + M)

Windows Key + ,: Temporarily show desktop

Connecting and Sharing

Windows Key + K: Connect to audio devices and wireless displays

Windows Key + H: Share content (if it is supported by the current app)

Windows Key + E: Open Windows Explorer

Traditional Keyboard Shortcuts

Windows Key + Shift + Left or Right: Move current Window from one monitor to another (when using a multiple monitor setup)

Windows Key + Space: Switch the input language of the keyboard (if you have included at least a second one)

Windows Key + 1, 2, 3, and so on: Open programs that are pinned to the taskbar

Windows Key + P: Project a screen

Windows Key + R: Run a command

Alt + Tab: Switch to the previous window

Windows Key + T = Cycle through screenshots of open apps

Alt + F4: Close the current window. If you do this combination when viewing the desktop, the Power dialogue will be opened to restart or shut down Windows, switch or sign out the current user or put your device in sleep mode.

5 Windows 10 Methods of taking Screenshots in

Screenshots are wonderful ways of documenting and sharing your screen's content. Be it a glitch that you are explaining to a tech support personnel, a tweet, or a hilarious autocorrect text, the ability to save your text for future use is useful.

Fortunately, there are different ways of capturing the screen. Widely known are the old methods of using the Snipper Tool for screen grabbing, Print Screen key for creating a new file, and other third party programs.

Taking a Screenshot of Your Entire Screen

1. Press the Print Screen button on the keyboard. The screenshot will be stored in the clipboard from where you need to paste it into a graphics editor like Windows Paint.

2. Type "paint" into the search bar.

3. Select "Paint"

4. Click "Paste"

Your screenshot is ready!

Taking a screenshot of only the Active Window

1. Press Alt + Print Screen.

2. Type "paint" into the search bar (if Paint is already open, click Control+N and click OK when Paint asks you to set the width and height).

3. Select "Paint"

4. Click "Paste"

The screenshot taken is just of the active open window!

Making a screenshot without a third party program

1. Press Windows key + Print Screen.

Your screenshot will be in the Screenshots folders of your pictures

Taking a Screenshot of a Specific Part of Your Screen

1. Type "snipping tool" into the search bar.

2. Choose "Snipping Tool"

3. Click "New"

Your screenshot is available in the Snipping Tool!

Taking screenshots with more Tricks

1. Enter the <u>download page</u> of PicPick click on "Free Download"

2. Carry out the installation instructions. You will see a menu for methods on how to capture a part or all of your screen. When you click "Scrolling Window" you will capture as many pages as you can scroll through instead of the whole static page.

3. The key command for screenshots for your computer will change when you install PicPick. So be aware of the commands. Click on the "Show hidden icons" arrow located in the bottom right corner of the screen.

4. Click on the PicPick's icon.

5. Select "Program Options"

7.   Select "Hotkeys" located at the left-hand menu.

From the above, you can see what the default commands have been modified to after installing PicPick. You can also change them to your preference.

Windows 10 Password Change

The following is how to change your password and protect your documents and files while using Windows 10.

Even if there is no very important stuff on your laptop, having a password on your Windows 10 is still very necessary. Microsoft provides three options to keep you safer. We have experimented on the three of them and laid out simple steps on changing your password.

For setting your password, we recommend making use of a combination of numbers, letters and symbols. It is also best if it has at least eight characters. Though we recommend alphanumeric passwords, we also advise that you change the format to that of a picture or pin with which you can sign in to your Microsoft account faster. Also, we advise that you use Chrome's incognito windows for more privacy

In addition Windows Hello, helps you to sign in to your account via fingerprint and facial detection. If it is the old school method that you prefer below is how to set your Windows 10 password.

To Set / Change your Windows 10 Password

1. Click the Start button located at the bottom left of the screen.

2. Click Settings from the list located on the left side.

3. Select Accounts.

4. Select Sign-in options from the menu.

5. Click on Change under Change your account password.

7.   You have to sign in with your Microsoft account password before you can change the password. Input your password in the box and click Sign in.

8.   A new code to change the password will be sent to you via the phone number connected to your account. Input the last four digits of your phone number to ascertain that it is the correct number then Press Enter.

8. Enter the code that comes to your phone.

9. You will be directed via a new page to input your old password and also input the new password. Then Reenter the new password and press Enter.

The message below will be displayed if you are successful!

Change Your Password to a PIN

1. Carry out the four steps under the To Change Your Current Password guide above.

2. Click on Add under PIN located in the sign-in options.

3. To change your password, you need to sign in to your Microsoft account. Input your password in the box and Click Sign in.

4. Input a new pin in the first box and enter it again in the second box then click OK. You can now make use of this pin to sign into your Microsoft account.

Change Your Password to a Picture Password

1. Carry out the four steps under Change Your Current Password above.

2. In the Sign-in options, click on Add located under Picture Password.

3. Input your Microsoft account password to verify that it is your account then click OK.

4. Click on Choose Picture and select a photo from your file list.

5. If you see a picture that you like, click on Use this picture, click on Choose new picture if you do not see any. You can position your picture any way that you want by dragging it.

6. Your picture password will have three gestures that you have to set up. You will have to set up three gestures that will become part of your picture password. Draw circles or lines with your cursor that will coordinate with your photo. I drew three spikes in the statue of liberty's crown as seen in New York.The message below if displayed means that your password creation is successful. The photo that you set will show up when you want to sign in to your Microsoft account. Just redraw your already set gestures to sign in to your account.

Uninstalling Windows 10 programs

Uninstalling software is one of the most performed activities by users in a computer system. However, Windows 10 first time users may find programs difficult to uninstall. Just like in Windows XP and 7, the control panel menu and the Programs and Features still exist in Windows 10 but these will not delete most of the new software.

However, there is a simple way of removing this software, whether is a Universal app a Windows 8-style Modern app. Below is a guide on how to uninstall Windows 10 programs even if you don't know the type of software it is.

1.Enter the Start menu.

2.Click Settings.

3. Click System located in the Settings menu.

4. Select Apps & features located at the left pane.

A list of all the apps installed in the computer will be displayed in the right pane.

5. Select the app that you wish to uninstall.

6. Click the Uninstall button that is displayed. System apps that you cannot uninstall will be greyed out.

7.Confirm your action by clicking the Uninstall button.

How to Include an Adult or Child User in Windows 10

Sharing your computer with family members entails everyone having his or her own login. Also, each user has their own Start menu, desktop layout and data folders. You can also include a child account which will restrict the apps and the websites that the child visits while reporting their activities to you. The below is a guide on how to include adult and children accounts in Widows 10.

1. Go to Settings. You can access the settings menu from the Start menu.

2. Click Accounts.

3. Click Family & Other Users located in the left window pane.

4. Click either "Add someone else to this PC" or "Add a family member". After that select "family member" if you are adding either an adult that needs the access to parental controls or you an adding a child. If there are no children making use of the system then you can select "Add someone else . . ".

3. Click Finish

Changing the Windows 10 Screen Resolution

Changing the Windows 10 display resolution is not difficult to understand and perform. The options include changing from a lower resolution to a higher resolution and also changing back to the default size. Whatever it is, we have got you covered.

The below is the guide on changing your display resolution. It is ideal to select the display size that is recommended and also modify your icons and fonts and to your preference.

1. Navigate to the Start button.

2. Click the Settings icon.

3. Choose System.

4. Select the Advanced display settings

6. Select the option of your choice. We suggest that you select the option having (Recommended) next to it.

8.   Click Apply.

Once you have correctly done all these then you have successfully changed your display resolution!

Synchronizing your iPhone and Windows 10

Though iPhones work better with Macbook, it does not mean that it cannot work with Windows 10. The synchronization process with Windows 10 requires a little know-how unlike that of macOS. Nevertheless, a little more knowledge and patience will help you achieve your aim.

Copying to an iPhone

Syncing photos, movies, TV shows and music requires interactions with iTunes. If you are already making use of it then you are one step ahead. If you are not, download it here, then import your music into iTunes by going to File > Add Folder to Library. Follow the steps below ones you are done with the above..

1. Use a lightning cable to connect your iPhone to your laptop.

2. If the computer displays a prompt asking to have access to the phone then Click Continue.

3. Click the phone icon located in the top bar.

4. Click Sync.

Doing these should successfully sync both devices. If it does not, navigate to the sidebar and enable the checkboxes under sync for Apps, Movies, Music, TV Shows, Photos and Apps then click Sync again.

The size of data that you are syncing determines the time it will take.

5. Check to ensure that your videos, apps, music and photos, have entered your phone.

Using your voice to control Windows 10

Depending on the user, the Voice Control can be a hit-or-miss. Nevertheless, it is an easy way to perform tasks faster. There are built in voice controls for certain apps in Windows 10 such as Cortana, where it is used to answer questions fast and make quick searches.

Let's get started on setting up Windows Speech Recognition and also exploring Cortana's abilities.

1. Go to the Cortana search bar and type Windows Speech, then click Windows Speech Recognition to enter it.

2. A pop-up window will be displayed. Click Next to continue.

3. Choose your microphone, then press Next. A separate microphone or headset is your best bet in getting the best result. System with built-in mics will still work fine.

4. For a guide on how to place your microphone, follow the instructions displayed on-screen, then press Next.

5. Follow the displayed prompt to calibrate the microphone, then press Next.

6. For your computer to understand you better when you speak, select whether to let your computer review email and documents.

7. Select an activation mode.

When you say "Stop Listening" with the voice activation mode, the Windows Speech Recognition will turn off. Alternatively, you can select the key combination (CTRL + Windows) to deactivate or activate this feature.

9.   To easily access the commands that Windows understands, Print the speech recognition card. You can also save this link to view later.

10.   When you startup the system, select whether you want to run Speech Recognition. If you don't, you will have to do it manually via the control panel.

11.   Finish the setup by viewing the tutorial on knowing more about the abilities of Speech Recognition.

Adding a printer in Windows 10

There are many short-time activities that you can do to improve the use of your computer be it customizing your action center or speeding up the boot time of hour computer. When you install a printer in Windows 10, it allows you to quickly print documents after you must have set them up. The below is how to install a printer in Windows 10.

Commonly, connecting a printer to your computer is by USB. This makes it a local printer. Also, you can add a printer to your network that is connected to another computer or install a wireless printer. The below guides cover these scenarios.

Add a Local Printer

1. Using the USB cable, connect the printer to your computer and switch it on.

2. Go to the Start menu and Open the Settings app.

3. Click Devices.

4. Click Add a printer or scanner.

5. When Windows detects your printer, click on the name of the printer then follow the instructions displayed on the screen to complete the installation.

If your connected printer cannot be seen by Windows, click the link written: "The printer that I want isn't listed".

When you do this, the Windows troubleshooting guide will help to locate the printer. It will also search for and download the drivers for the printers.If it does not still work, go to the website of the manufactures and download the tools for installation and drivers of the printer.

Add a Wireless Printer

The procedures for wireless printer installation differ between manufacturers. Despite this, it is common for modern printers to automatically detect the printer and get ready for installation

1. To enter the wireless set up, make use of the printer's LCD panel. This is located at Setup > Wireless LAN Settings on my Epson printer.

2. Choose your Wi-Fi network. Also needed is the SSID of your home network. You can find this by hovering over the Wi-Fi icon with your mouse.

3. Input your network password.

Some situations require you to connect your printer to your computer temporarily with a USB for the software installation. Automatically, your added printer will be located in Settings > Devices.

If you encounter any problems, ensure that your printer is not far from your wireless router and also close to your computer. If your printer is making use of an Ethernet jack, you can directly connect it to your router and also use a browser to manage it.

Add a Shared Printer

HomeGroup which is Windows' home networking feature automatically shares some files and printers with the other computers that are in the home network. We will showcase how to set up HomeGroup and also connect to a shared printer.

Set Up a HomeGroup

You can skip this step if your home network is already setup and has a HomeGroup ready. Otherwise, follow the first and second steps below to do this.

1. Right-click on the wireless icon located in the taskbar and choose "Open Network and Sharing Center".

2. Click "Ready to create" which is next to HomeGroup. If there is an existing HomeGroup, it will inform you by displaying "Joined."

3. Click the Create a homegroup button.

4. Click Next.

5. Choose the items that you want to be shared. By default, Printers & Devices are already shared.

6. Write down the HomeGroup password that Windows creates for you. It will be needed for any computer wanting to join the HomeGroup.

7. Click Finish.

Customize Windows 10

Modify the Windows 10 UI to look like how you want it. You can adjust the icon size, change the theme or make the OS into a dead ringer for Windows 7.

Tapping a tile with your finger or using your mouse to click to open a Windows app is a waste of time. The keyboard shortcut is the fastest and least physically demanding method of opening an app. Windows 10 lets you make custom shortcuts for any app, be it a "universal app", "desktop app" or Window 8's "metro apps". This is how to do it.

Method 1: Creating a Desktop Shortcut

1. Launch the command prompt window. Type "cmd" in the Search or Cortana box to get there. Then right-click on Command Prompt and choose "Run as administrator."

2. Type "explorer shell:AppsFolder" (without quotes) in the command prompt and press Enter. A window with a list of all your apps will be displayed.

3. Right click on an app and choose Create shortcut. Changing the view to "detailed list" can help you find your app easily as they all will be in one column.

4. Click Yes when a prompt is displayed, asking you if you want the shortcut to be on the desktop. When you do this, the new shortcut icon will appear on your desktop.

5. Right click on the new shortcut icon and choose Properties.

6.   Enter a key combination in the Shortcut key field. The combination has to be CTRL + ALT + a number / letter.

7. Click OK.

Note: Remember that you should not make use of the same key combination two times. Also, note that there are programs that make use of the CTRL + ALT + keyboard shortcuts which will also launch in their windows. As an instance, pressing CTRL + ALT + I in Photoshop Elements displayed the reside menu.

Method 2: Use the Start Menu

You can create shortcut straight from the Start Menu if you are making the shortcut for any desktop app. This is basically any app that is installed directly instead of via the Windows Store. Using this method helps you avoid creating a different shortcut icon for the desktop.

1. Open the Start Menu.

2. Navigate to the app icon that you want. If the app is not displayed as a tile, you can locate it by clicking on All apps and scrolling through the list.

3. Right click and choose Open file location. Doing this open a window having the icon of a shortcut. If Open file location is not displayed on the menu, it means that it is a universal or modern app. Therefore you have to do the first method above.

4. Right click the shortcut icon and choose Properties.

5. Input a key combination in the "Shortcut key" box.

7.   Click OK.

Creating a new folder in Windows 10

Is better organization needed for your documents and files? Then you need to group your related files into specific folders in your laptop so that you can easily locate them whenever you need them. You can also change the icon size to improve the viewing. Below is a fast way to create new folders in Windows 10. You can also learn protecting your Windows 10 folders with a password .

Method 1: Using keyboard shortcuts to create a New Folder

Utilizing the CTRL+Shift+N shortcut is the quickest method of creating a new folder in Windows.

1. **Go to the location where you want to create the folder.** You can make a new folder in any location of your hard drive or inside another folder in File Explorer. You can make use of this method to create a folder on your desktop.

2. **Simultaneously press down the Ctrl, Shift, and N keys together.** Shen you do this, Windows will create a folder with the folder name "New folder."

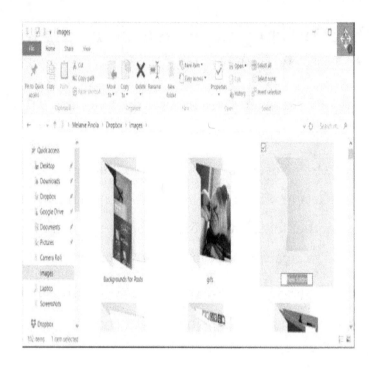

3. **Input your preferred folder name.** Creating a folder using this method takes just some seconds. Ensure that you rename the folder to what you want because it will still bear the "New folder" tag if you do not rename it.

Method 2: Right-click to create a new folder

If you like making use of the mouse or you do not remember the keyboard shortcut:

1. **Go to the location where you want the new folder to be.**

2. **Right-click on a blank spacethere**. Be careful when doing this because you will be presented with the wrong menu if you right click on a file.

3. A menu will be displayed, **Select New then Folder** when it does.

After doing this, Windows will create a new folder there.

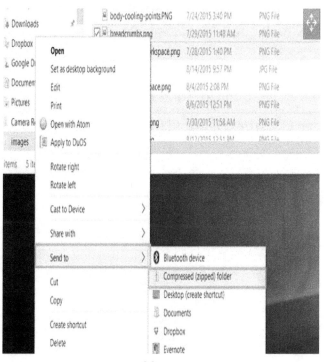

4. **Input the name you want** to replace the "New Folder" tag. Then press Enter.

You can also make use of this method to create folders on the Desktop. Just right click on a blank space on the Desktop, and click on New, then Folder.

Method 3: Create a New Folder from the Ribbon Menu

An alternative way of creating a new folder is to make use of the New folder button that is located in the File Explorer menu.

To do this, go to the location that you want the new folder to be, then click the "New folder" located in the Home tab

Besides the methods explained above, you can make use of the Command Prompt to create a new Windows 10 folder. To do this navigate to the location where you want the folder to be then type mkdir foldername. Replace the "foldername" with your preferred name. However, these methods are the fastest and easiest ways of creating a new folder in Windows 10.

Ways to make Windows 10 look similar to Windows 7

Compared to Windows 8, Windows 10 has improved features. These include the ability to make use of Universal apps, Xbox game streaming, better wake-from-sleep and boot time, and the Cortana voice assistant. Also, it has the Start menu which is glaringly missing from Windows 8. What if you like the performance of the Windows 10 but prefer the feel and look of the Windows 7. Even though you cannot make everything look identical, you can still modify some elements like the taskbar, wallpaper, and the Start menu.

I. Install a New Start Menu

The Start Menu is present in Windows 10, and it is very different from the previous ones. Unlike the previous ones where a list of apps will be displayed upon clicking, the Start button here displays a set of live tiles and frequently used apps on its left side. You can not pin an icon as you would in Windows XP and 7 but you can include live tiles. Thankfully, you can install a custom Start Menu that functions and looks the way you like. There are many Start menus out there, which are Windows 10 compatible but we prefer Classic Shell due to its customization.

1.**Download and install Classic Shell** version 4.2.2 or higher. For this article, we made use of 4.2.2 which is available for download at the Classic Shell forums. The earlier versions do not work well in Windows 10.

2.**During the process of installation, deselect Classic IE and Classic Explorer.** Deselect you as you can still try using them, but we do not find them very useful.

3.

Enter the Classic Start Menu settings. If the Classic Shell is already running, a Shell icon will be displayed at the lower right corner of the screen. Right-click it and choose Settings. On the alternative, just search for "Classic Start Menu Settings."

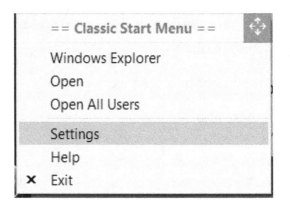

4.

Tick the Show All Settings box if it has not been already ticked.

5.

Go to the Start Menu Style tab and choose Windows 7 Style if it has not been already selected.

6.

If you want the Start button to look real, go to <u>this thread</u> and **download the image of the Windows 7 Start button**. Many custom buttons are available there. After that go to the **Start Button tab and choose a Custom button to search for the image.** Ensure that the Show All Settings box is ticked to see the Start button tab.

7.

Go to the Skin tab and choose Windows Aero from the pulldown menu.

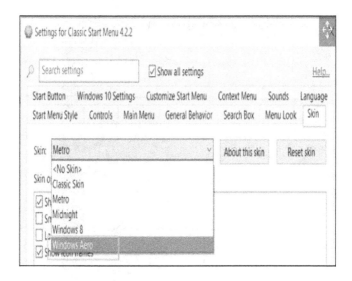

8.

Click Ok for your Start Menu to look like this.

II. Conceal the Search/Cortana Box

A search box is prominent on the taskbar of Windows 10.
When clicked, it brings up Cortana. Though it is useful, you
may want to remove it. Besides, when you install another
Start menu or the Classic Shell, it comes with another search
box. Do the following to conceal the Cortana box:

1.

 Right-click on the search box for a context menu to be
displayed.

Changing the Windows 10 default font

You can change the default Windows 10 don't, Segoe to your preferred choice by tweaking some registry settings. Doing this will also change the fonts for Windows 10's menus, icons, File Explorer, title bar text, and others.

The first thing to do is to backup your registry setting to allow you to reverse your settings anytime you want. After that, just update the registry with a .reg file.

1. **Press Win+R.**

2. **Type regedit and click Enter.**

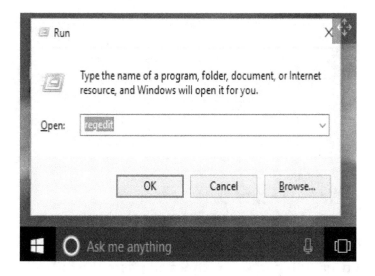

3. To save the registry file on your hard disk, **Go to File > Export**.

4. **Enter Notepad then copy and paste the following to it:**

Windows Registry Editor Version 5.00

[HKEY_LOCAL_MACHINE\SOFTWARE\Microsoft\Windows
NT\CurrentVersion\Fonts]
"Segoe UI (TrueType)"=""
"Segoe UI (TrueType)"=""
"Segoe UI Black (TrueType)"=""
"Segoe UI Black Italic (TrueType)"=""
"Segoe UI Bold (TrueType)"=""

"Segoe UI Bold Italic (TrueType)"=""

"Segoe UI Historic (TrueType)"=""

"Segoe UI Italic (TrueType)"=""

"Segoe UI Light (TrueType)"=""

"Segoe UI Light Italic (TrueType)"=""

"Segoe UI Semibold (TrueType)"=""

"Segoe UI Semibold Italic (TrueType)"=""

"Segoe UI Semilight (TrueType)"=""

"Segoe UI Semilight Italic (TrueType)"=""

[HKEY_LOCAL_MACHINE\SOFTWARE\Microsoft\Windows NT\CurrentVersion\FontSubstitutes]

"Segoe UI"="Verdana"

To use as your system default, replace the Verdana located in the last line with the name of your preferred font. To search for the correct and full name of your preferred font, open your Fonts folderby typing Fonts in the search box.

5. **Click File > Save.**

6. **Change the "Save as" type to "All Files."**

7. Give the file a .reg extension in the filename field.
Name it anything you like as far as it ends with the .reg
extension.

8. Click Save.

9. To run, **double-click your just created registry file.**
When you do this, a prompt will be displayed seeking your
permission to allow changes to the computer. When it is
successfully done, you will get a confirmation.

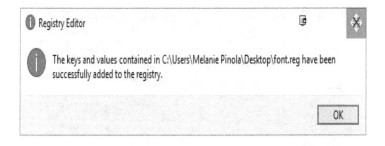

The keys and values contained in C:\Users\Melanie Pinola\Desktop\font.reg have been successfully added to the registry.

OK

10. To see if your changes have been effected, **restart your computer**.

As a warning, do not change the default change to fonts like Wingdings, if not your system will be unreadable.

Turning off System and Notification Sounds in Windows 10

Each newer Windows version brings better notification features but can still be annoying to users. This guide shows how to turn them off and use the notification window which slides out from the screen's bottom right.

- **Click the notification icon** located on the screen's bottom right. You will see it at the toolbar's far edge, next to the time and date.

2. **Click the All Settings** icon located in the bottom right.

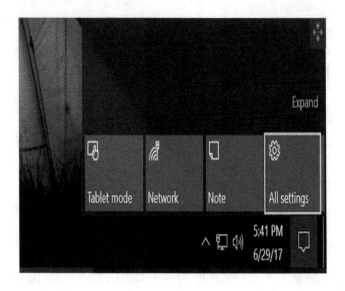

- Select **System** from the screen of the main Settings screen.

- Choose **Notifications &actions** in the left sidebar.

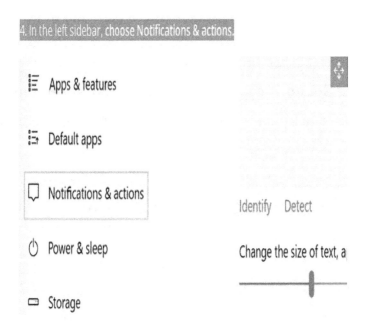

- Slide the button for **Get notifications from apps and other senders to the Off position** to turn the Notifications completely off.

Notifications

Get notifications from apps and other senders

 On

Show notifications on the lock screen

 On

6. To disable just the notifications that you select, scroll down to the **Get notifications from these senders section,** then choose one from the option: **sounds, banner or neither.**

Changing your Windows 10 desktop background

Though the blue Windows 10 wallpaper is beautiful, it is better to set a background of your choice on your laptop. Also, you should consider changing the size of your icon , and choosing one from the array of Windows 10 lock screen images as wallpaper options. For extra customization, try activating Light Mode or Dark Mode and changing to any of these beautiful themes.

Going further, the below is how to change your Windows 10 desktop background.

1. **Click the Windows icon** in the screen's lower left located next to the search bar.

2. A list will be displayed, **click on Settings** in the list.

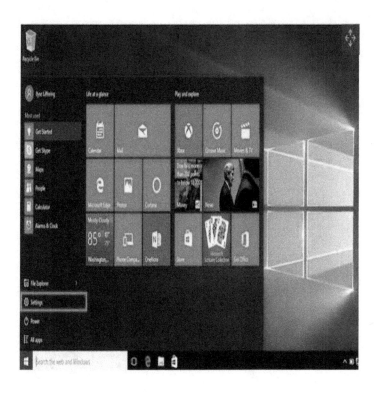

MORE: How to Use Windows 10 - Guide for Beginners & Power Users

3. **Click on Personalization**, which is the fourth item at the bottom of the list.

4. **Click on Background**. The background page will be displayed to allow you to preview your background picture and allow you to choose different pictures and use them as the background of your desktop.

5. **Click on the box below Background** to select either a slideshow, solid color, or a picture.

6. Below Choose your picture, **click any of the options** or **click Browse** to select one from your computer. Click on whatever photo you want and it will appear as your desktop background.

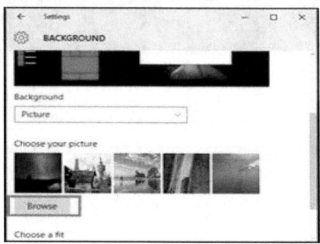

- You can **click on the box located below it** if you do not like the picture's layout. Then pick from any of the following to **select a fit** for your background: fit, tile, stretch or fill.

- The background of your Windows 10 screen will automatically change according to your selection.

Changing Windows 10 Icon Size

Do you want your <u>Windows 10</u> desktop icons to be bigger so that you will stop straining your eyes or be easier to tap on a <u>touch screen laptop</u>? Or do you want them smaller than your shortcuts will not take up much of your <u>laptop's</u> screen space? The steps below guide you on what to do.

1. **Right-click on empty desktop space**.

2. **Select View** from the displayed contextual menu.

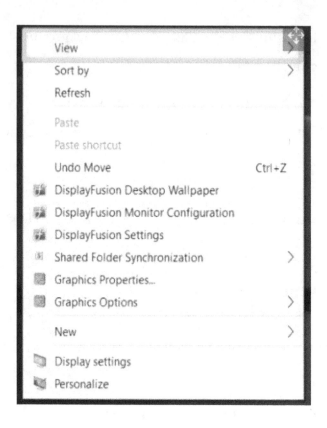

View	
Sort by	>
Refresh	
Paste	
Paste shortcut	
Undo Move	Ctrl+Z
DisplayFusion Desktop Wallpaper	
DisplayFusion Monitor Configuration	
DisplayFusion Settings	
Shared Folder Synchronization	>
Graphics Properties...	
Graphics Options	>
New	>
Display settings	
Personalize	

3. **Select either Small icons, Medium icons, or Large icons.** The default one is the medium icons.

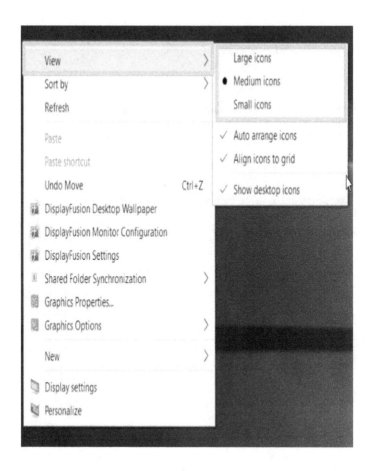

On my laptop with a native 1600 by 900 pixels display, the
large option looks huge, the small size is too small, and the
medium size looks just right (as Goldilocks would say). Your
mileage might vary depending on your screen's display
resolution. Changing the size of the icons on the desktop
doesn't affect the size of the icons elsewhere in Windows 10,
but there are ways you can change those too.

Changing the Taskbar Icons' Size

There is a different setting for changing the taskbar icons sizes. Doing this will also change the size of your Windows 10 apps, text, and other items.

1. **Right-click on empty desktop space.**

2. From the displayed contextual menu, **choose Display settings.**

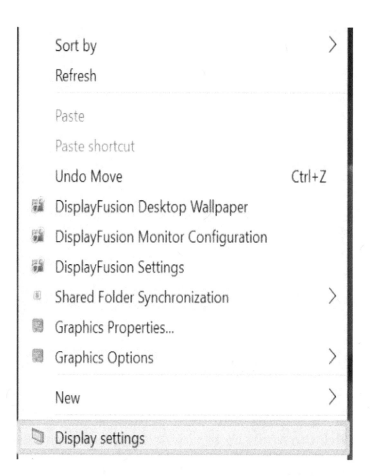

Sort by		>
Refresh		
Paste		
Paste shortcut		
Undo Move		Ctrl+Z
DisplayFusion Desktop Wallpaper		
DisplayFusion Monitor Configuration		
DisplayFusion Settings		
Shared Folder Synchronization		>
Graphics Properties...		
Graphics Options		>
New		>
Display settings		

3. **Slide the slider** located under "Change the size of text, apps, and other items" to 175%, 150%, 125%, or 100%.

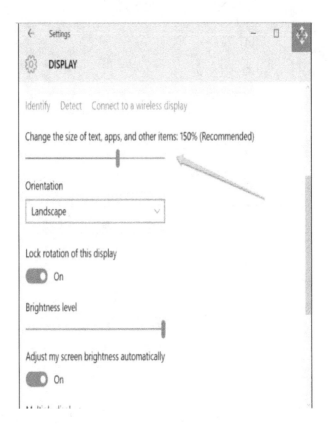

4. **Click the Apply** button located at the settings window bottom. To get a better experience, Windows may require you to log out and back in.

This will make the size of the taskbar icons as well as that of text in apps like Calendar, Microsoft Edge, and the notification windows.

Changing the File Explorers icon size

You can change the sizes of thumbnails or icons of specific folders via File Explorer.

Navigate to the location of your folder and zoom in or out using the scroll wheel of your mouse. This switches the view between Windows 10's small icons, medium icons, large icons, details, list, content, and tiles view.

Although File Explorer will remember your last setting when you open this folder again, this is a folder-specific setting, so you'll have to adjust each folder you would want a different icon and text sizes for.

Enabling Windows 10 Light Mode

There is a new light mode by Microsoft for those not comfortable with the Dark mode. Introduced in the May 2019 update is the Windows 10 new light theme which illuminates the interface.

This new light mode is the Windows 10 default look. This replaces the former UI that consisted of multiple dark features which include the taskbar. As a result, Windows 10 will by default appear transparent white across its apps and menus.

MORE: Giving Windows 10 a Dark Theme

Follow this guide to enable Dark Mode if you prefer the Dark mode. Also, if you are Google's browser user, you can enable Chrome's Dark Mode. Furthermore, follow this guide if you prefer creating your own theme, be sure to check out this breakdown of how to do so. You can also make mild random changes to the UI by learning how to customize your desktop background and also install third-party themes via the Windows Store.

Below is a guide on activating the Windows 10 light mode.

1. Navigate to the start menu at the screen's bottom-left corner.

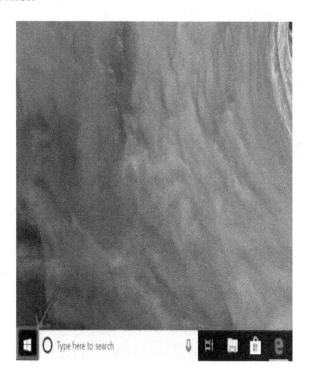

2. Click the **Settings icon** symbolized with a **gear**.

3. **Click on Personalization** from the Windows settings screen.

Windows Settings

Phone
Link your Android, iPhone

Network & Internet
Wi-Fi, airplane mode, VPN

Personalization
Background, lock screen, colors

Time & Language
Speech, region, date

Gaming
Game bar, captures, broadcasting, Game Mode

Ease of Access
Narrator, magnifier, high contrast

Update & Security
Windows Update, recovery, backup

4. Select **Colors** located at the left-hand sidebar.

Background

Background
Picture

Choose your picture

Browse

Choose a fit
Fill

5. Go down to the end of the page and select "**Light**" from the drop-down menu.

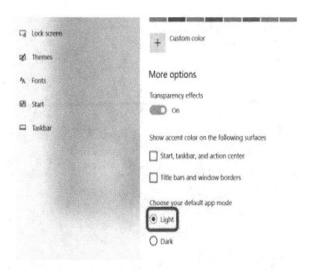

Enabling Windows 10 Dark Mode

The Dark mode is a prominent design that is becoming rampant in our mobile phones. Apple utilized the theme in macOS Mojave. Also, Google will soon introduce it to the Chrome OS and the Android Q. For Windows 10, the Dark Mode is a feature already present as Microsoft added it some years ago.

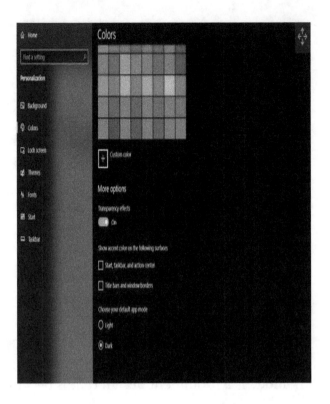

This feature changes the white spaces and colors of the UI, apps, and browser to black color. Some pages, tabs, and icons become either shadowy gray or black while the text becomes white for better contrast. If you still prefer the white theme, check out the Light Mode guide.

MORE: Using macOS Mojave's Dark Mode

Aside from its look, Dark mode also improves sleep and reduces eye strain. As a result, it is worth the try when you upgrade to the latest Windows 10 version. To assist you, we have compiled a guide on enabling Dark Mode on Windows 10.

1.Click the Start menu and select the gear icon to **Enter settings**.

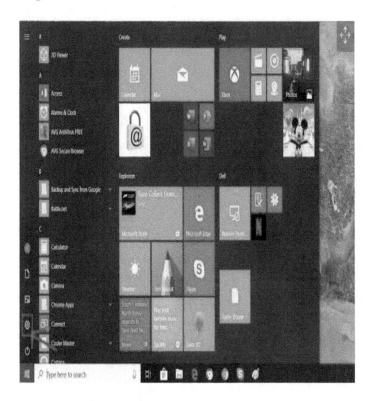

2. **Click the icon for Personalization**

Windows Settings

3. Click the **Colors tab** located on the page's left side.

4. Scroll to the page's end and navigate to the "**Choose your default app mode**" menu and select **Dark**

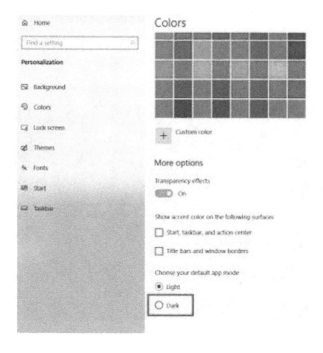

Hiding your Email Address and Name on the Login Screen of Windows

While using a Microsoft account for your computer login, Windows reveals your email address and real name on the login screen. This can pose privacy issues especially from people looking over your shoulders while you are making use of your laptop publicly. This is less secure when comparing it to entering your password and username. However, below are two methods of hiding your info from the login screen.

The procedures below work for both Windows 8 and Windows 10 and will also be applied to all your PC's user accounts. Note that you will have to make use of the registry method if you are making use of Windows because it does not allow you to access the Group Policy Editor.

First Method: Hide your user information by editing the Computer Policy

1. Search in the Windows taskbar for "Local Group Policy Editor" and press Enter.

2. Go to Computer Configuration > Windows Settings > Security Settings > Local Policies > Security Options.

3. Double-click on "Interactive logon: Display user information when the session is locked". This feature informs Windows

about the information to display on the login screen anytime your laptop is not unlocked.

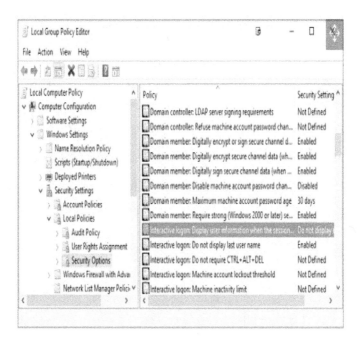

4. Choose "Do not display user information."

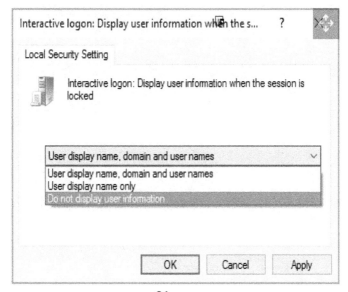

5. **Click Apply, and then OK** for it to be immediately effected.

6. After that **double-click on "Interactive logon: Do not display last user name".** This feature informs your Windows whether it should show your user information when your computer is booted up.

- **Click OK after changing the settings to Disabled.**

Restoring the My Computer icon on Windows 10

Though Windows 10 improved certain features, it however still altered some other features that many users have become used to. One such feature is the My Computer icon on the desktop which is missing in Windows 10. Nonetheless, we have a way of bringing it back.

This procedure also teaches you how to bring back other icons you may want to bring back. Here is how to do it:

1) **Right-click on the desktop and choose Personalize.**

2) **Click Themes.**

3) Click "Go to desktop icon settings."

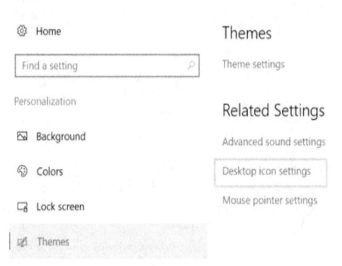

4) **Tick the box that is next to Computer.** Also, you can tick the boxes for User's Files, Control Panel and Network if you want to take them to the desktop.

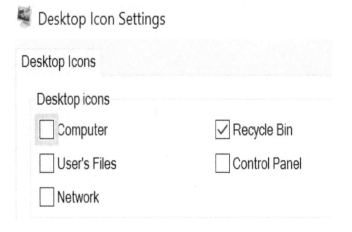

5) **Click Apply.**

6) **Click OK.**

7) **Right-click on This PC.**

8) **Select Rename.**

9) **Type "My Computer."**

10) **Click Enter.**

Adding Another Column to the Windows Start Menu

By default, Windows 10 displays only three tile columns in the Start menu. There is a fourth column that displays more apps and info if you click the Windows button. This is how to activate it.

1. **Open Settings.**

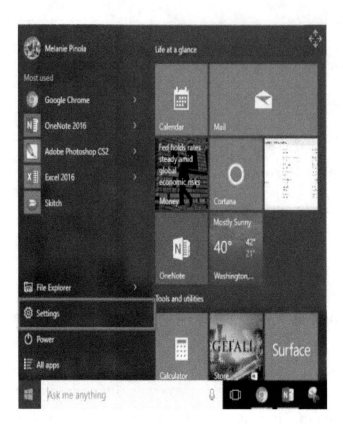

2. **Click Personalization.**

3. **Click Start located in the left menu and then put it on by toggling the "Show more tiles"**

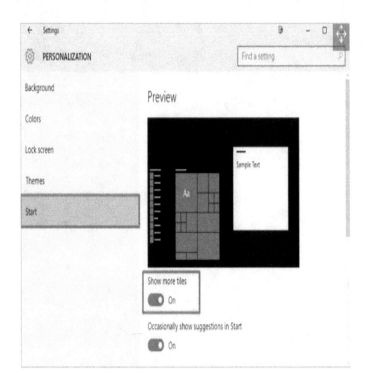

When this is done, the Start menu will now feature an extra space for which you can drag tiles to fill.

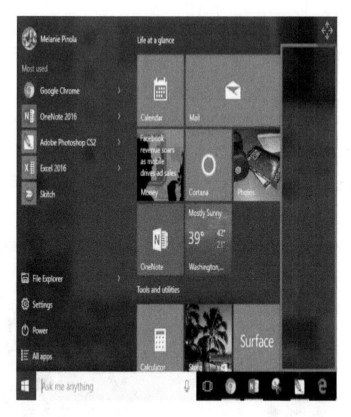

Also, you can get an additional four tile columns for more organization if you drag the Start menu's edge to the right.

Editing pictures to fit your Windows 10 display

It is not satisfying to see the cropped out pictures Windows 10 applies anytime you set a picture as your desktop background or lock screen. Thankfully, this can be modified to fit your display.

This can simply be done on your PC. Just navigate to the image that you want to make use of and carry out the following:

1. **Navigate to the image in Photos and move the cursor over the window's top.**

2. **Click Edit.**

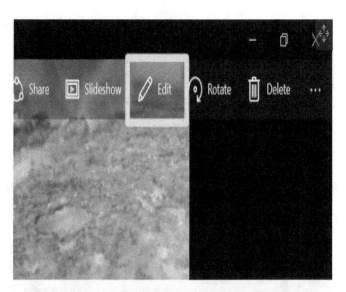

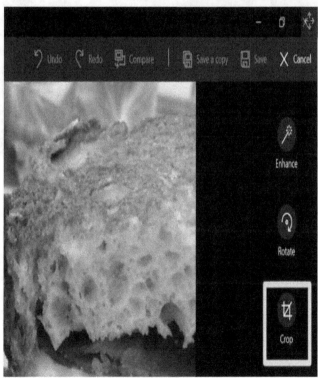

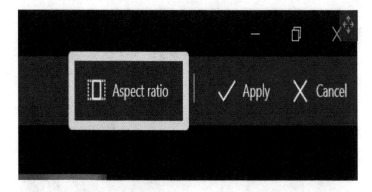

5. Choose Lock Screen.

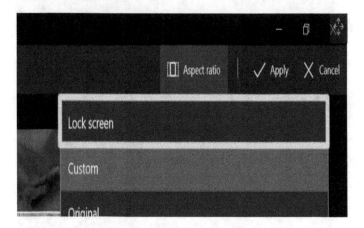

6. Drag the corner dots of the crop box to adjust it and choose where you want to use, then click Apply.

- **Click Save a copy.**

- **Click the ... button.**

- **Choose Set as.**

- **Choose either Set as background or Set as lock screen.** Redo the steps 8, 9 and 10 as many times as necessary.

If you properly carried out the steps, then you have successfully cropped your picture to your display size!

Finding the Spotlight Lock Screen Images of Windows 10

By default, Windows 10 Spotlight feature should display beautiful images by Microsoft on the lock screen if enabled. The pictures range from beautiful cities in the world to nature images. Also, the pictures occasionally rotate. However, what can you do if you find and want to keep an image you list from the catalog. The pictures are buried deep in your directory, so finding them requires some digging around before you can save them and make them your wallpaper.

Nevertheless, here is how to go about it:

Finding Windows 10's Lock Screen Images

1. Go to File Explorer and **click View**.

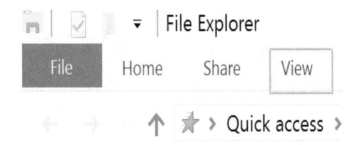

2. **Click Options.**

4. Select "Show hidden files, folders and drives" then click Apply.

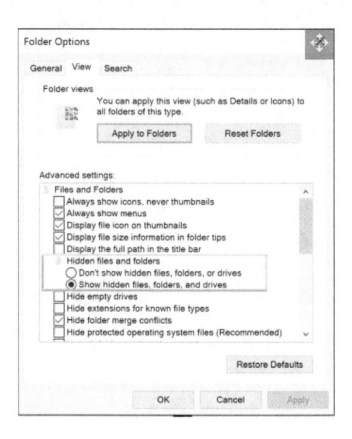

5. Navigateto **This PC > Local Disk (C:) > Users > [YOUR USERNAME] > AppData > Local > Packages > Microsoft.Windows.ContentDeliveryManager_cw5n1h2tx yewy > LocalState > Assets**

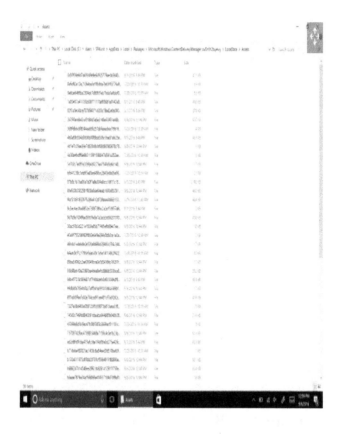

A large list of file names will be displayed which makes little or no sense and shoes no extensions. There is no better method of finding which picture is which than click on the ones with bigger file sizes.

6. **Copy the most recent large files to another folder** (ex: images).

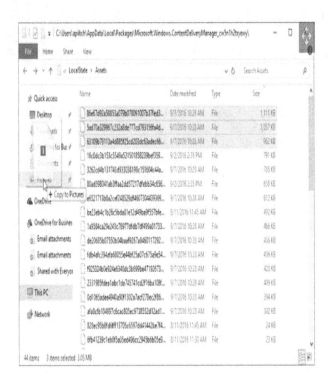

- **Rename the files then add the extension .jpg** to the name's end.

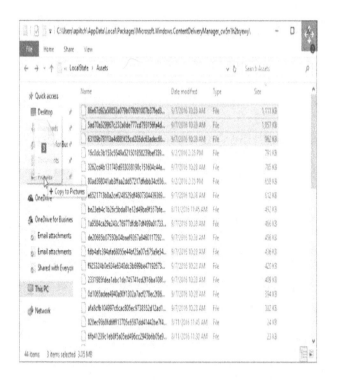

After doing this, the pictures should now be visible to be viewed in any image editor or viewer.

Also, note that Windows can add and remove any of the pictures whenever it likes. So grab and save the ones that you like immediately.

Customizing the AutoPlay Menu of Windows 10

A pop-up requesting your next line of action is normally displayed anytime you slot in an external hard disk, DVD, USD Drive, or other media into your computer. This feature is called AutoPlay. Just like me, you may find it irritating. Just follow the steps below to turn it off. Also, you can still customize its reaction to different media.

Below is the guide for customizing Windows 10 AutoPlay:

Disable Windows 10 AutoPlay

1. **Navigate to Settings > Devices.**

2. Click AutoPlay located in the sidebar.

3. To switch off, toggle off the "Use AutoPlay for all media and devices" button.

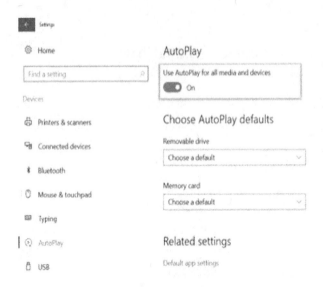

Pick Specific Actions

1. **Enter** the Control Panel.

2. **Select AutoPlay.**

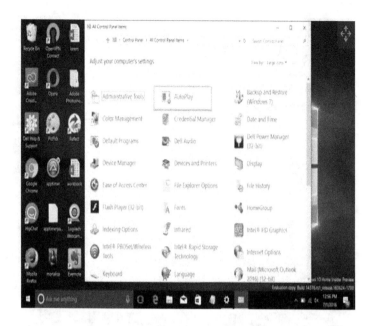

Here you can decide the reaction of the files and drive when
you insert a media. Click **Save** when you are done.

Installing and Deleting Windows 10 fonts

Just a limited number of fonts are available in Windows 10.
Most graphics and publishing apps install their fonts when
you download and install them. However, if you really want to
make your documents and artwork distinct you will need
some of yours. Below is a guide on installing, deleting and
searching for new Windows 10 fonts.

Location to Find a Font

For now, there are 3 main fonts that Windows 10 work with. They are PostScript, OpenType and TrueType. There are several sites where you can get more fonts but we prefer Google Fonts because it comes with many free type faces. Most of the best fonts come with a price tag, however, you get most of them at Microsoft's typography site and Fonts.com .

Installing a Font

1. Go to Google Fonts or any other site and **Download your fonts**. Then save them in a folder. Unzip them in they are in the .zip format.

2. Go to the Cortana search box and type "**fonts**".

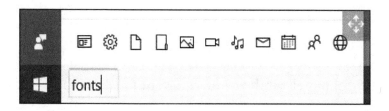

3. Displayed in the result list is the **Fonts control panel icon**. Click it.

A control panel window with different fonts will be displayed.

4. **Enter the folder that you downloaded** the uninstalled fonts. If you downloaded them to the Downloads folder, press Windows + E to go to File Explorer and choose Downloads from the menu.

5. Drag the fonts to the window of the control panel fonts. Be informed that you cannot drag folders that are font-filled, instead, you have to drag the fonts alone.

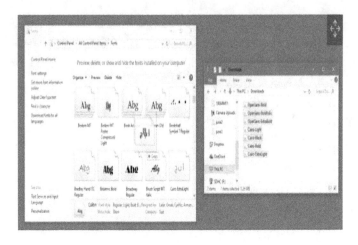

Deleting Fonts

You can easily delete fonts taking up your hard drive space.

1. **Go to the Fonts window.** Just as earlier stated, you can just type "fonts" in the search box and select "Fonts: control panel."

2. **Select the font family or font** that you want to delete. If it just a font that you want, it may be located within a "font family". As a result, you have to open it by double-clicking. To illustrate, Cambria Bold is listed in the Cambria family.

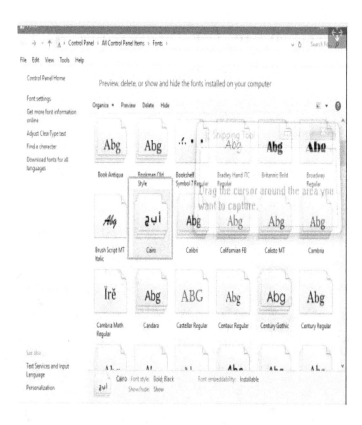

3. **Press the delete key.**

4. **Click Yes** when a warning is displayed.

Customizing the Windows 10 Action Center

The Action Center of Windows 10 proffers an efficient way of accessing the different options that the PC has. However, the default setup may not be convenient for you. Fortunately, cleaning up the Action Center is easy as it presents your required buttons and also in your required preference order.

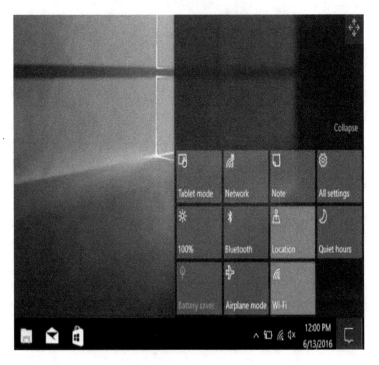

This cleaning process can be very helpful since the user can either conceal the Project button or position the Tablet Mode button in an easier to locate place. The below is how to customize the Windows 10 Action Center.

MORE: Using Windows 10

1. Click the Start button.

2. Click the Settings icon.

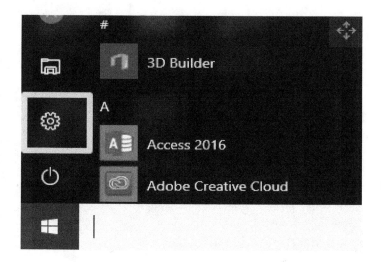

3. Click System.

Windows Settings

Find a setting

System
Display, notifications, apps, power

Devices
Bluetooth, printers, mouse

Network & Internet
Wi-Fi, airplane mode, VPN

4. Click Notifications & Actions located at the left menu.

5. Drag and drop the Action buttons.

6. Click "Add or remove quick actions."

- **Turn the Quick Actions off or on** to conceal them in the Action Center.

Doing these customizes the Action Center.

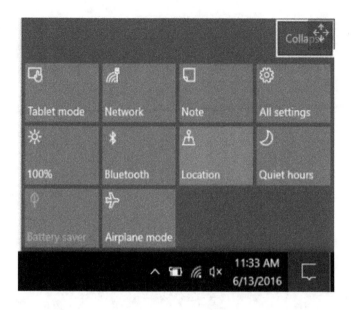

Enabling Windows 10 Spatial Sound

One wonderful feature rolled out with the Windows 10 Creators Update is the ability to get a better audio experience with headphones. The feature, Spatial Sound gives headphones a kind of 3D effect, one that is similar to true surround sound, though depending on its source.

By default, this feature has been disabled. But the below guide showcases how to enable it.

- **Right click on the sound icon** located at the bottom right side of the system tray.

- From the context menu, **choose Playback devices**.

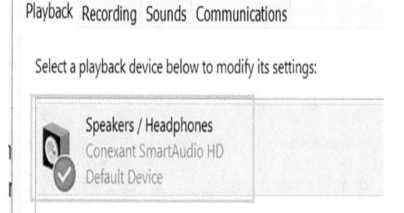

2 Click the speaker type or headphones that you would want Spatial sound enabled on.

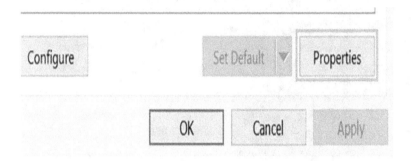

3 Click the Properties button located at the bottom right.

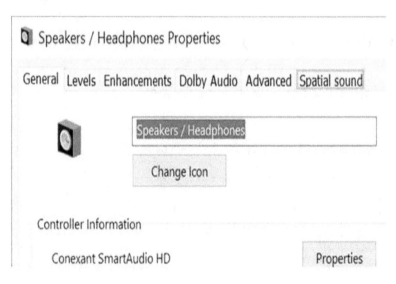

4 Select the Spatial Sound tab located at the top.

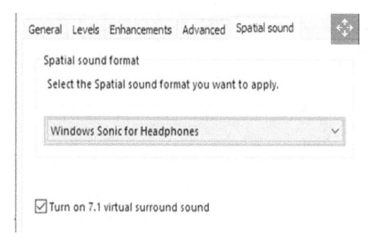

General   Levels   Enhancements   Advanced   Spatial sound

Spatial sound format

Select the Spatial sound format you want to apply.

Windows Sonic for Headphones

☑ Turn on 7.1 virtual surround sound

5From the displayed dropdown menu, **choose Windows Sonic for Headphones** (if it is for a speaker, choose other).

6 When your done **click the OK button.** <ok.png>

Pinning a Website to the Start Menu of Windows 10

The Start Menu is back in Windows 10 with Live colorful Tiles and a familiar interface. Through the Start Menu, users can easily access content and apps, and at the same time is given easy access to options for customization.

The Edge browser which is Microsoft's new browser allows you to pin websites to the Start menu. This keeps you one click away from accessing latest updates and news. Below is how to go about it.

1. Navigate to Edge.

2. Go to the site that you want to pin.

- **Click on the three-dot menu button** located at the top right.

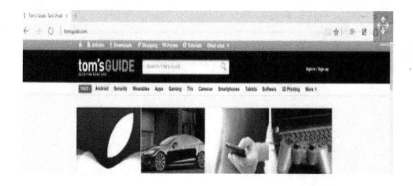

- **Choose Pin To Start.**

When you are done, you should be able to see the site pinned in the Start menu anytime you press the Windows key.

How to Resize or Unpin the Tile of a Website

1. Enter the Start menu.

- **Right-click the icon** of the page that you want to unpin.

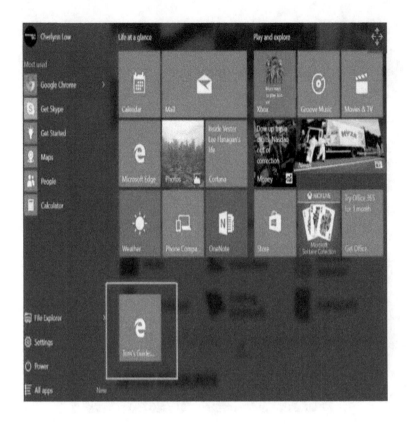

- **Select either Resize or Unpin From Start**.

Fix Problems

Windows 10 is enjoyable but can be annoying sometimes.

Learn how to speed up a slow-opening Downloads folder,

disable or speed up a personalized ads, rotate your screen, fix

issues by booting into your BIOS, prevent the OS from

restarting to update when not given the permission to and also how to run older programs in the compatibility mode.

Repairing and Restoring Windows 10

You can fix your Windows 10 if it boots but crashes midway or doesn't load at all. Also, you can easily fix a rotated screen. You can make use of the power settings to speed up your laptop booting if it is slow to boot. That said here are a few guides for Windows 10 repair.

First Step: Use Windows Startup Repair

Your first point of action is to use Startup Repair if you noticed that your Windows 10 is difficult to boot and takes you to the desktop or the login screen. Here's how:

1. **Go to the Advanced Startup Options** menu of Windows 10. On most laptops, pressing F11 when you boot up the computer will take you to the Windows 10 Advanced Startup Options. Another alternative is to boot via an install disk and press Next > Repair.

Choose Troubleshoot when your computer has booted

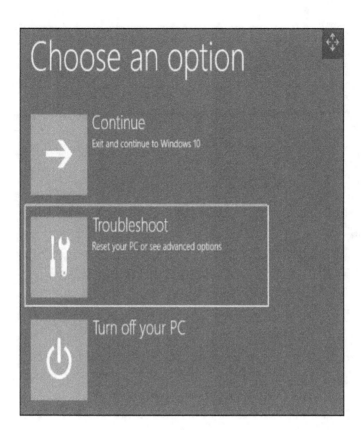

Then click Advanced options.

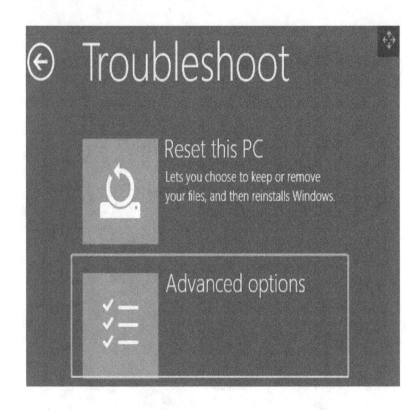

2. **Click Startup Repair.**

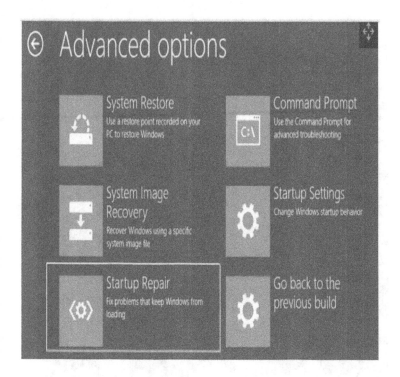

You will need to exercise some patients as Windows takes its time to fix the problem. It may or may not be successful in fixing the issue.

Second Method: Use Windows Restore

1. Finish the first step from the previous procedure on how to **get to Windows 10's Advanced Startup Options menu**.

2. **Click System Restore.**

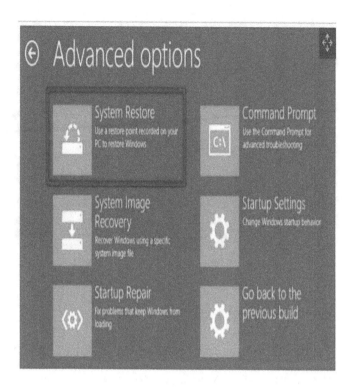

The computer will reboot.

3. **Choose your username.**

- Input your password.

- From the menu, **choose a restore point** and carry out the displayed instructions. You can make use of the method below if you do not have a restore point.

Disabling the Windows 10 Lock screen

Anytime that your computer wakes from sleep or boots, you have to swipe up or click the mouse for the lock screen to disappear and present you with the login interface.

Disabling the lock screen to go straight to the login interface can save you some precious time. Here is how to do this:

Enter the registry editor. Press CTRL + R and type regedit in the prompt then press Enter.   If you get a warning from the User Account Control, Click Yes to confirm.

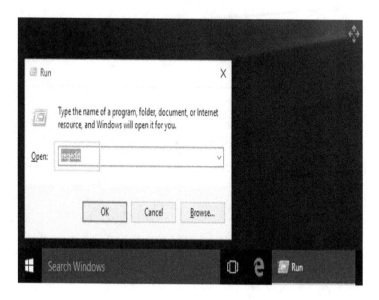

2.

Open the folders in the tree

HKEY_LOCAL_MACHINE\SOFTWARE\Policies\Microsoft \Windows.

3.

If there is none available, **Create a new registry key called Personalization**. To do this, right-click on the right pane and select Key, then rename it to "Personalization."

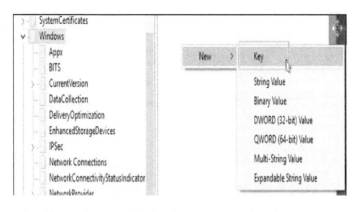

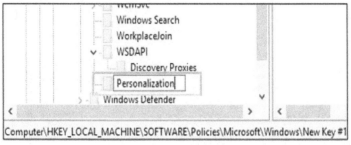

Computer\HKEY_LOCAL_MACHINE\SOFTWARE\Policies\Microsoft\Windows\New Key #1

4.Navigate to the Personalization key.

5.Right click on the right pane and click New then DWORD (32-bit) Value.

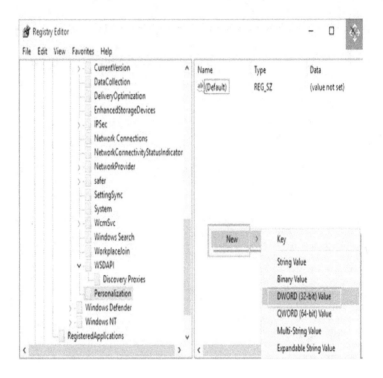

6.

Name the new value "NoLockScreen" (without the quotes).

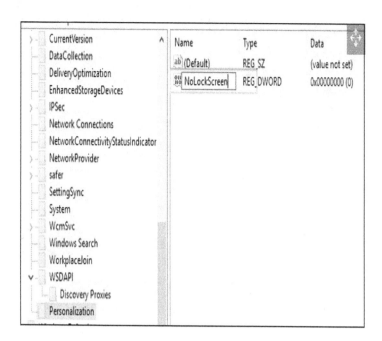

7.

Double click on the name then input "1" in the Value field to set **NoLockScreen to 1**. Then press OK.

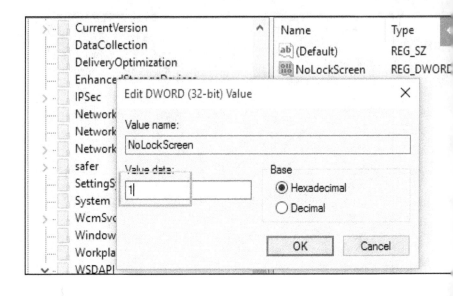

Setting Compatibility Mode for Windows 10 Apps

Some software that was created for previous Windows versions work well in Windows 10, but some do not work well or even don't work well at all. You can fix these issues by simply changing the settings of their compatibility mode. Also learn how to open a port on Windows Firewall if you still having issues.

The Windows built-in tool called Program Compatibility Troubleshooter automatically fixes compatibility problems. You can make any app run in compatibility mode if the troubleshooter cannot fix the problem. This will make the run the settings of its earlier Windows version. You can make the troubleshooter automatically search for apps with issues or manually run the troubleshooter for the specific app. Here is how to carry out both actions.

Using Windows' Program Compatibility Troubleshooter

1. Go to the taskbar search box and **enter run programs, then click "Run programs made for previous versions of Windows."**

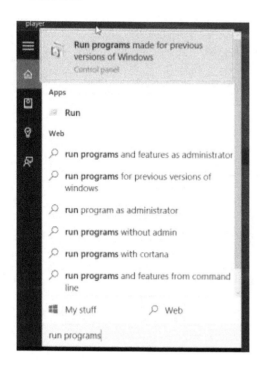

2. **Click Next**, then the troubleshooter will try to detect the app issues.

3. In the next window, **click on the app**, then **click Next.**

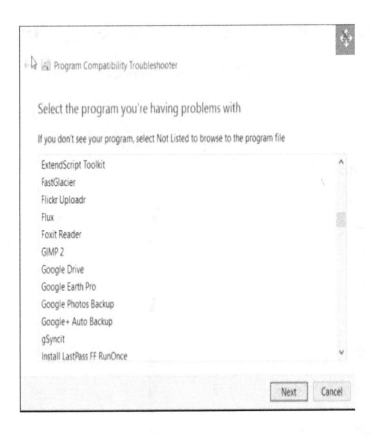

4. Select a troubleshooting option: Select the compatibility settings that are recommended. You can still choose your compatibility settings.

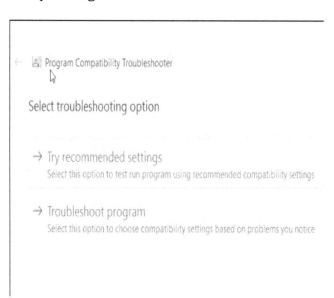

If you select the settings that are recommended, the troubleshooter will use a previous Windows version to run the app to try and fix the issue.

If you choose to manually troubleshoot the app, the troubleshooter will ask you about the problems that you are facing. Depending on what you select, the troubleshooter will give problem-solving suggestions such as testing the app display settings.

5. Click the Test the program button and click Next.

You can choose to either report the issue to Microsoft to see online helpful articles or save the app settings.

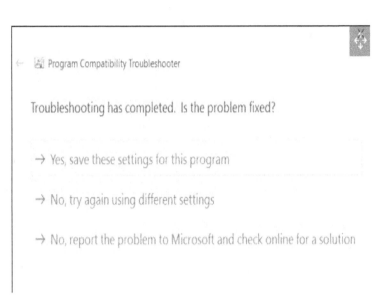

You will have to run the troubleshooter for the app that you are having a compatibility issue with.

MORE: <u>Windows 10 Settings You Should Change Immediately</u>

Running an App in Compatibility Mode

As an alternative, you can change the app's compatibility settings by accessing it via its properties. The compatibility mode allows you to force an app to make use of earlier Windows settings for that app. You can also change the app's color and display settings.

1. **Choose Properties afterRight-clicking on an app.** This can be done via the EXE file in the file browser or via the shortcut for the app.

2. **Choose the Compatibility tab, then tick the box that is next to "Run this program in compatibility mode for:"**

3. In the dropdown menu, **choose the Windows version** that you want to use for the settings of the app.

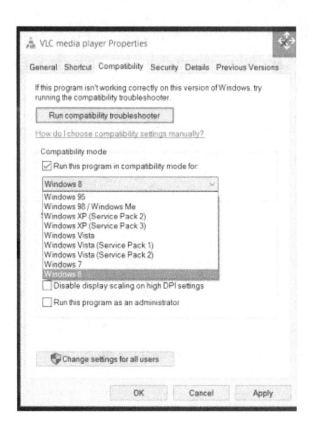

4. **Press Apply**, then **open the app** to see if the issues are fixed.

Restarting Windows 10 Without Rebooting

Having to restart Windows to add a new app, install updates or fix issues can be annoying. Fortunately, there is an easy activity to perform of which you do not have to restart the computer at all. Instead, it will temporarily stop Windows, then force it to reboot. Once this happens, the computer will think that it was rebooted, it will then continue as normal.

- **Press CTRL + Alt + Delete** or **Right-click the Start menu**.

- **Choose Task Manager**. <manager.png>

- **Look for Windows Explorer** in the process list.

System			1.4%
System interrupts			0%
Windows Explorer			0%
Windows Logon Application			0%
Windows Session Manager			0%
Windows Start-Up Application			0%

- **Right click and select Restart**.

Services and Controller app	0%	0.2 MB	0 MB/s	0 N
Shell Infrastructure Host	0%	0.5 MB	0 MB/s	0 N
System	0.4%	0.1 MB	0.1 MB/s	0 N
System interrupts	0.1%	0 MB	0 MB/s	0 N
Window:	0%	2.1 MB	0 MB/s	0 N
Window:	0%	0.1 MB	0 MB/s	0 N
Window:	0%	0.1 MB	0 MB/s	0 N
Window:	0%	0.1 MB	0 MB/s	0 N

Restart
End task
Resource values >
Create dump file
Go to details
Open file location
Fewer detai Search online
Properties

Ways to locate the apps or processes draining your laptop battery

If you notice your battery going flat faster than it should, it probably means that there is an app that is using bigger power than expected. Luckily, the Windows Battery Saver utility can display the breakdown of your battery usage.

Even though Chrome has a history of draining the battery, other little know apps drain the battery too. Thankfully, the Battery saver will help you locate them too. This tool also helps you regulate the apps that should be functional in the background.

Below is the guide for locating what is draining your laptop's battery and also regulate your background apps.

- **Click the Start button.**
- **Choose Settings.**

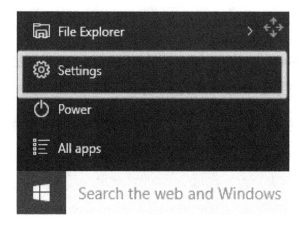

- **Click System.**

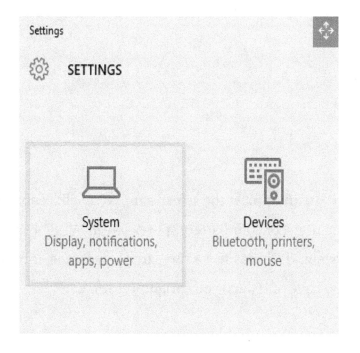

- **Select Battery saver.**

- **Select Battery Use** to view the break down of your battery usage per app.

- Toggle on the Battery saver to limit your app's background activities.

Overview

Battery life remaining:
94%

Estimated time remaining:
5 hours 22 minutes

Battery use

Battery saver

Extends battery life by limiting background activity and push notifications.

Battery saver is currently:

Off

Battery saver will turn on automatically when your battery falls below 20%.

7. **Click on an app.** At the screen's top, you will be able to view the usage of your battery split between Wi-Fi, Display, and System. If Display has a very large percentage, it means that you have to reduce your brightness level.

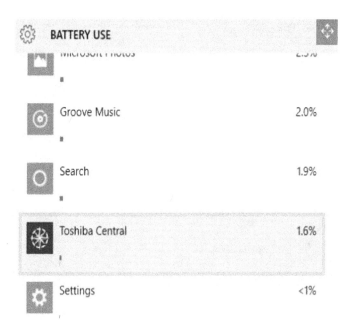

- **Click Details.**

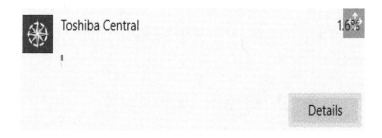

8. **Switch off the "Allow this app to run in the background"button** to make it consume less of your battery power.

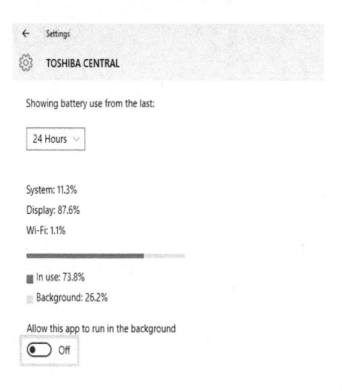

Hopefully you now know how to keep your battery less drained.